Singer Come from Afar

Singer Come from Afar

poems

Kim Stafford

Red Hen Press | *Pasadena, CA*

Book layout by Daniela Connor

Library of Congress Cataloging-in-Publication Data
Cover photograph by Kim Stafford

Names: Stafford, Kim Robert, author.
Title: Singer come from afar : poems / Kim Stafford.
Description: First edition. | Pasadena, CA : Red Hen Press, [2021]
Identifiers: LCCN 2020049841 (print) | LCCN 2020049842 (ebook) | ISBN
  9781597098885 (trade paperback) | ISBN 9781597098878 (epub)
Subjects: LCGFT: Poetry.
Classification: LCC PS3569.T23 S56 2021 (print) | LCC PS3569.T23 (ebook)
  | DDC 811/.54—dc23
LC record available at https://lccn.loc.gov/2020049841
LC ebook record available at https://lccn.loc.gov/2020049842

The National Endowment for the Arts, the Los Angeles County Arts Commission, the
Ahmanson Foundation, the Dwight Stuart Youth Fund, the Max Factor Family Foundation,
the Pasadena Tournament of Roses Foundation, the Pasadena Arts & Culture Commission and
the City of Pasadena Cultural Affairs Division, the City of Los Angeles Department of Cultural
Affairs, the Audrey & Sydney Irmas Charitable Foundation, the Kinder Morgan Foundation,
the Meta & George Rosenberg Foundation, the Albert and Elaine Borchard Foundation, the
Adams Family Foundation, the Riordan Foundation, Amazon Literary Partnership, the Sam
Francis Foundation, and the Mara W. Breech Foundation partially support Red Hen Press.

First Edition
Published by Red Hen Press
www.redhen.org

ACKNOWLEDGMENTS

Thanks to the editors of the following magazines where some of these poems first appeared: *Adventures Northwest, Open Spaces, Orion, Pilgrimage, Poetry, Salamander, Sojourners, Terrain, Texas Monthly, Windfall,* and *World Literature Today.*

Some of these poems first appeared in a series of chapbooks from Little Infinities Press: *Circumference: Poems of Consolation, December's Children: A Month of Daily Writing, Dr. Fauci's Smile: Pandemic Poems, Earth Verse: Poems for the Earth, In Praise of Disarray: Poems of Love & Affection, Meditations & Poems for Writers, Peace Warrior: Poems in English & Spanish, Reunion of the Rare: Poems of the Oregon Territory, The Flavor of Unity: Post-Election Poems.*

"Advice from a Raindrop" first appeared in *A Generous Nature: Lives Transformed by Oregon,* by Marcy Houle (Oregon State University Press, 2019).

"Blue Brick from the Midwest" first appeared in *Oregon Quarterly,* and later (as did "How I Came to Be") in the chapbook *Prairie Prescription,* by Kim Stafford (Limberlost Press, 2011).

"*Dastgah*" was published in *World Literature Today,* and included as part of an audio program performed by Michael Meade.

"Earth Totem" first appeared in *For the Love of Orcas,* ed. Andrew Shattuck and Jill McCabe Johnson (Trail to Table, 2019).

"Nuptial Flight" first appeared in *If Bees Are Few: A Hive of Bee Poems,* ed. Jim Lenfestey (University of Minnesota Press, 2016).

"Pandemic Coffee Restoration Ritual" was posted in the elevators at Good Samaritan Hospital in Portland, Oregon.

"Shelter in Place" was printed in *Calligraphic Coronavirus Chronicles,* a collection of poems as a benefit for the Oregon Food Bank by calligrapher Carol DuBosch, 2020.

"Two Arab Men" first appeared in *Healing the Divide: Poems of Kindness and Connection*, ed. James Crews (Green Rivers Press, 2019).

And several of the pandemic poems have appeared in the Portland *Oregonian*, have been read on the radio, reprinted in nonprofit newsletters, and distributed informally via neighborhood poetry posts.

CONTENTS

I.

In Spite of War

2.
Pandemic Poems

3.
Revising Genesis

4.
The Cup No One Can See

5.
And All My Love

1.

In Spite of War

White Flag Patriots

The children went first
because they had the most to lose—
no color, no emblem on their flags,
no shouting, surrendering instead
as they shuffled toward the White House,
some crying, some stern,
a few humming lullabies
their mothers had taught them.

In the Rose Garden, where men
babbled into microphones,
the children lay down in the grass
to watch clouds drift west
until speeches trailed off
and only the wind was heard.

Then white flags flashed
as the children rose and sang together,
You have overcome, but we are not afraid.

For the Customs Agent Who
Seized Claudia's Jar of Honey
from El Salvador

for Claudia Castro Luna

Para probar, she said. Taste it. Let it
sizzle on your tongue. Take it home
smuggled in your dark pocket,
and with a spoon drip to the tongues
of your children slow sips of joy
so they may know how sweet
my country once was in spite
of war and sorrow. Tell them
about the ravine of flowers
the soldiers missed but the bees
swarmed, humming and humming,
zumbando y zumbando.
Remind them how a mother
could sit by the road with
her daughter in her arms
and a few jars of true gold,
how my coins in her brown
hand meant enough this day,
even though her man was gone,
even though your law would take
this elixir from me, even though
there will always be war, but always
flowers, bees, mothers, and your children.
If you have no children, if you do not wish
to think of war, or my country, or the woman
by the road, still, I beg you, taste this honey,
let the sticky song of a thousand bees
give your body the oldest, deepest pleasure.

Do not lose your chance to know
how sweet my country once was
in spite of war and sorrow,
a pesar de la guerra y el dolor.

Nest Filled

Use your whirling wings to find the right tree.
Use your pert eye to choose the level limb.
Use your nimble feet to cherish the hospitable fork.

Use your fearless beak to gather twigs, leaves,
grass and thistledown to weave your basket-house
open to the wuthering sky.

Use your body to be the tent over tender pebbles,
lopsided moons. Then wait—warm, alert, still
through wind and rain, hawk-shadow, owl night.

Use your life to make life, spending all you have
on what comes after. And if you are human, a true
citizen, fully awake, then learn from the sparrow

how to build a house, a village, a nation. Use instinct
to find the right place. Use thought to know the right
time. Use wisdom to design the right action.

In the era of stormy weather, build your
sturdy nest, and fill it with the future.

Dear Mr. President

In sheer contradiction of your efforts
to warn our fellow citizens of the danger
of immigrants, a certain Antonio—from
Michoacán, who has been living without documents
as my neighbor for fifteen years—has put me
to shame with his work ethic, thrift, good humor,
and courage, building stone walls, repairing roads,
tilling gardens, and otherwise inflicting beauty
and good order on this neglected corner of our nation
in spite of all you say to drive him away.

You, sir, are not getting through!
He keeps smiling, and bending to any task
we offer for simple wages, humming a song
I can't get out of my head or heart.

I do not know how to advise you, sir.
You have labored long and loud to cast him
down, cast him out, but he just keeps
humming that song: *Qué linda está
la mañana, en que vengo a saludarte. . . .*
He is saying the morning is beautiful,
sir, and he greets you, singing.

The Flavor of Unity

El sabor que nos hace unidos.

The flavor that makes us one cannot be bought
or sold, does not belong to a country, cannot
enrich the rich or be denied to the poor.

The flavor that makes us one emanates from the earth.
A butterfly can find it, a child in a house of grass,
exiles coming home at last to taste wind off the sea, rain
falling into the trees, mist rising from home ground.

The flavor that makes us one we must feed
to one another with songs, kind words, and
human glances across the silent square.

Old Glory's New Red, Black, and Blue

Cue the anthem, slide down the flag
that flew through World Wars I and II,
then assailed Korea, Vietnam, Afghanistan, Iraq,
and now a hundred nameless places where drones
look down on weddings to seek out villains known
or guessed—old wars and new, the flag flown high
to woo our crew to action for our banner blue, our
devotion true—until money tattered it as inequality
grew, and drew us, first a few, then more, to view
in new light the plain hue of white one clue
a change was due—so beat the drum's
tattoo and raise anew our flag
of red, black, and blue.

Sunset red, shadows blue and black, indigo
and scarlet *deja vu* when dew falls heavy
in the grass to strew starlight in diamonds
through the dusk. No stew of sorrow at our
rendezvous. No one to misconstrue this change
as anything but patriotic on the avenue of many colors
hitherto passed over when some hullabaloo, some retinue
of old privilege and this fresh generation's overview
began to see a world askew and must eschew
old privations and renew our love of freedom
to pursue our happiness and make taboo how
certain citizens because of color were subdued,
so bring forth now the red, black, and blue.

Brew a bold libation, fire up the barbecue,
and offer feasting *cordon bleu* to celebrate

what no judicial review, no internal revenue, no
voodoo Waterloo from here to Timbuktu can make
untrue, what no zoo of caged freedoms can deny
some citizens have been held second class in lieu
of rights by law but yet false in fact. We say
adieu to that. We're all in one canoe, our ship
of state that flies the banner red, black and blue.

Now we must interview each other, give our leaders
one stern talking-to, root out each residue of prejudice,
outdo old talk with questions and with follow-through,
hew the righteous line and find in black all colors joined,
all ethnicities of shade and blend and flavor, so may good
accrue. For we were gathered from one Genesis when God
threw galaxies together spinning with diversity *beaucoup*.
In keeping with that old creation, we must now imbue
our politics (that have been one big bugaboo) with kindness
to us all at last, undo each miscue that slew our honor
so may ensue a tart *fondue* of plenty. We stir
the *roux* of flavors in our bold debut: Old Glory
dressed up now in red, and black, and blue.

Blue and black—this the color of a bruise: no news
to those who made the Blues, and something no-one could
confuse with anything but hurt. So set the Statue of Liberty
at Standing Rock to face down opposition to democracy,
wealth flowing corrosive through pipes of steel to spew
into the river collateral trouble for the Water Keepers
who knew Pilgrims were first refugees, seeking freedom
for faith first welcome to these shores. Does our dream
arc toward justice still? Can we call that effort true,

supreme, or is our legacy sunk to pay-per-view?
We must fly the red, the black, and blue.

This mighty woman, mother of exiles with a torch
who lifts her lamp beside the golden door shall dress
her copper in these colors now to call this century's
huddled masses in. Her beacon-hand reveals that
at our best we are the watershed where myriad
streams are harvested, rivulets gathered into one:
Asian, Eurasian, African, Bedouin, Islander, Blue-
Blood Black, and every lovely shade of brown,
from dark dusk to sand, and every hue of Wanderer
or Fugitive from darkness seeking light, every Indian
to this ground restored by right, for this we fight,
for this democracy our aspiration's light, for this
to be true, we will pledge allegiance now
to the red, the black, the blue.

Breast Milk, Ash, and the Needle

When first I learned to write my name there were doves
dancing in the dust by the shadow of the fig tree.
Grandmother guided my hand and on my paper
the line turned as the doves turned—a loop, a swivel,
and there I was: *Shaimaa.*

Slaves of Isis now, we will be sold. I must prick a wrist
tattoo, my name so family will know my body when it is
dumped beside the road. Milk from the nipple of my sister
here, from ash on the floor, and with this—this needle
that once stitched blossoms on the scarf of our mother.
Again: *Shaimaa.*

Before the guards wake, pain of the pricking by a spot of light
rescues me from sorrow so vast it keeps my breath from filling.
I prefer this little hurt, I prefer knowing I write to those who
loved me, lost me, fear for me, but they will read all I have
to say to them, of who we might have been when they
find this name: *Shaimaa.*

Maybe my uncle will drive and see the heap, and wonder,
and stop, and turn me over. I have been sold so many times
the sins of the soldiers have covered me like a mountain.
But he, a good man, folding my arms across my chest
will see the name, and weep: *Shaimaa. Shaimaa.*

Someday, this war will be a chronicle. My living sister will be
in it, and her boy. They will tell how our grandmother cried out
as I was dragged away over the door our father had made,
then in splinters across the floor.

They will tell how our mother prayed in silence for him, for me,
for all our cousins who are gone. Maybe there will be doves then,
in the flicker of shadows when they say my name again:
Shaimaa. Shaimaa. Shaimaa.

Do Not Follow Me

On this night before my execution I write you, my nephew:
do not follow me. Take care of your brothers. After tomorrow,
I am your life. See the sun for me. Be kind. Give bread.

Do not seek dark warriors who took me
from my work to make of me a number, a notch,
one bullet's worth of killing, burning, burying.

I will be gone, never to be found. But follow me then
with the wings of the first bird you see,
follow me into the rain's long corridor.

Do not follow to find me here in hell. Do not
chase rumors of my disappearance, clues to my
secret cell, as if you could save me from these.

But follow me into a face wherever you see it,
into a whisper, a song, a child's glance,
one hand holding another.

Do not take the path of fury or revenge that goes
in circles, where angry men are so afraid they spiral
until they shoot each other in the back—

a neat round hole where their names disappear
like smoke. Do not expect to find anything
but anger in the camp of anger.

But follow me into the flame of a candle at prayer,
wavering because a thousand miles away someone spoke
a soft word, and that little puff of air

traveled all the way unseen through the enemy camp,
across the desert, sure as a pilgrim going home
to find you, to touch your shoulder, your cheek.

That will be me. Follow me into the mornings
I will never see, but you see for me, days
when we will again be a country of children

and mothers, busy with their reading and laughing,
of fathers working among olive trees, where
the family cow settles in straw at sunset.

Do not follow me. I will be dead to them
but not for you. Be who I was in who you are.
Remember who we are. Be kind. Give bread.

Dastgah

A wandering musician from afar
arrives on foot, dusty with the journey,
and quietly performs while strolling
the strange city, steps lightly alone

through crowded bazaar, traffic-choked
knot, sings a snatch of old song, hums
a rising scale that climbs through tenements,
threads the seething kink of honk

and curse, sings through smoke, strums
through rank despair that billows
from money rubbing on pain,
in order to hear, follow, and find

any other wandering player in the thick of it
also strumming *oud*, tapping *tabla*,
breathing trill into reed pipe so pure
it can be heard through all this

human din—until one by one
the players convene and begin to braid
one rhythm into the next, salt harmony
and honey dirge, operatic scale rising

through sorrow to the pinnacle joy
that could lullaby the lost and waken you.

Presidential Alert

THIS IS A TEST
of the National Wireless
Emergency Alert System
No action is needed

This is your President speaking
Please take no action
This is only a test
Please remain calm
and silent

The National Wireless
is invisible and everywhere
Please take no action
No need to be alert
Who says this is an Emergency?

Just because I have your number
No action is needed
This is only a test
of what I can do
if I choose

No action is needed
Please be silent
I am in favor of no action
No need to be alert
THIS IS A TEST

New House Rules

In order to get beyond impasse,
Congress has replaced debate
with a listener's furthering response:

You sound upset . . .
I see . . . that makes sense . . .
Tell me more about that . . .
I'm sad to hear your pain . . .
Let me see if I'm understanding . . .
How does this make you feel?
Have you felt this way before?
Say again what you just said—
I need to understand.
How can I help?

Practicing the Complex Yes

When you disagree with a friend,
a stranger, or a foe, how do you
reply but not say simply No?
For *No* can stop the conversation
or turn it into argument or worse—
the conversation that must go on, as a river
must, a friendship, a troubled nation.
So may we practice the repertoire
                    of complex yes:

Yes, and in what you say I see . . .
Yes, and at the same time . . .
Yes, and what if . . . ?
Yes, I hear you, and how . . . ?
Yes, and there's an old story . . .
Yes, and as the old song goes . . .
Yes, and as a child told me once . . .
Yes. Yes, tell me more. I want to understand . . .
     and then I want to tell you how it is for me.

Repeat Offenders

Adverse conditions facing repeat offenders:
abuse, trauma, bereavement, mental illness,
poverty, homelessness, addiction.

—*news report*

Blame this man for being poor,
for his word "Lost" on cardboard.
Judge this woman for her pain,
how she sits so sullen.

Jail this boy child, old enough to go to war,
for schizophrenia, for PTSD, ranting
unable to stop, to simply be for one moment.
Look past his mother's addictions

her father beat into her brain so she
can't refrain from wanting somehow out.
Resent this old man's homelessness,
laid off forever, folded in a doorway.

Round up these veterans again and again
for all they lost again and again
in the jungle of their alleyways.
Rely on their bruises and scars,

those you can see, and those they hide,
to keep you safely above their pain.
Cripple compassion or it will cripple you.
Don't think or you will think too much—

the kind of thinking that invades a mind
sleepless under a bridge spooked by failures

far past midnight, a movie that won't stop.
There are so many sins, you can count them

every night, like counting sheep
until you pass out, pass through the ring of fire.
The sin of poverty. The sin of trauma.
The sin of killing for your country.

The sin of being so tender, so human,
you crumple into this disfigured hunch.
If you think too much, look too close, consider
the city of the hurt inside the city of the lucky,

you won't know what to do, what to believe,
how to get through a day without denial.
Isn't this what government is for,
what police are for, what laws are for—

to make those people those people,
and to make us us?

First Lady

She wept, they say, when he
prevailed, and not for joy.

She wished she could spend
her holiday on a deserted isle.

When he went to Switzerland
she visited the Holocaust Museum
solo, staring at the heap of shoes
while the Secret Service guys
tried to look busy, and
to disappear at the same time,
taking their cue from her.

Oh how we wish this cup
could be taken from her lips—
that the sun shine on her isle
and she weep for joy.

Equinox: Greta at Katowice

Because they were rich and clever, all
the ambassadors designed an echo chamber
of glass and platitudes, and took turns denying
the future. And because they were old, only
the next few years mattered, and so they pushed around
tarnished words like chess pieces in their narrow grid:

progress, growth, stability—

words any child could see were obscene, were
a screen obscuring catastrophe. So Greta stood
and showed them what maturity looks like,
what truth sounds like,
what leadership feels like,
and then she went home to change us.

Two Arab Men

Up out of the Metro at Clignancourt
we weave through the seething throng:
the old man holding a clutch of sunglasses,

the man with a forearm of ten watches,
another with a festoon of leather purses
in green, purple, brown, and crimson

all crying their wares in voices
bereft of hope—then the gauntlet
of stalls with jeans artistically ripped,

shirts fluttering their flags of fashion,
African masks, digital gizmos,
many offers, few sales, but then

the heart of peace appears when
two men step into the bright halo
of friendship, lean in to touch

head to head, right, then left, then
forehead to forehead, the close ritual
of what truly matters, deep economy

where the only currency is kinship.

Learning to Be

Trees wear their snow with grace.
Earth drinks the rain that falls.
The river turns at trouble, and flows on.
When wind comes, the grass says *Yes, yes.*

We resist, struggle, suffer.
We dig, bulldoze, pave, and burn.
We make intricate tools of destruction
to poison the garden, defile the well.

Why not learn to stand our ground—
not with guns, but like trees growing
leaves and offering apples, saying
with the grass to one another *Yes, yes?*

All My Relations

I want to thank all my relations
for this chance to be on Earth
in her time of flourishing; to thank
the First People of this place, the
the Multnomah people, the Clackamas,
Molalla, Tualatin, and Chinook, to honor
their sovereignty in long and continuing
relation, still teaching us how we might
be here together; to thank my mother and father,
moon and sun, for setting me forth before
their own passing on; to thank my grandmother
who listened to me so eloquently I learned
to listen to my own heart and mind, to find
stories and songs there; to thank my family
and friends, and all citizens and travelers
who study and work for deeper kinship
in this place, with one another, and with
all creatures, one Earth, visible, palpable,
fragile, intricate, resonant, in need of our
better stories. I want to thank you
who have gathered to receive what I have
carried here—in hope that something
I have may meet something you need,
so all our relations may be strengthened
for the life we live together.

2.

Pandemic Poems

In Quarantine

After they furnished us mortality estimates
on a sheet to post in the hall, after they sealed
the doors, after they counted our days of water—
by megaphone from outside the perimeter—after
they locked the gate, and then drove away, after our
desperate questions had exhausted all our tears, after we
looked at each other, first with suspicion of contagion,
then with curiosity, and then with love, someone
found a guitar, remembered a song, and we all
got in a line, laughing arm in arm, and danced.

Mingling

Remember how we used to do it—
weaving through the crowd, brushing
shoulders, fingers touching a sleeve,
adjusting a lapel—first an old friend here,
then turn to banter with a stranger, finding
odd connections—"You're from *where?* . . . You
know *her!*"—going deeper into story there, leaning
back in wonder, bending close to whisper, secrets
hidden in the hubbub, as if in the middle of this
melee you have found a room and lit a lamp . . .
then the roar of the crowd comes back,
someone singing out a name, another
bowing with a shriek of laughter,
slap on the back, bear hug void
of fear? Imagine!
Just imagine.

Spring Fever in Lockdown

From home, my room, long afternoon—
school never looked so good—even waiting
for the bus in the rain. Give it to me! No seat?
I'll stand, I'll stumble at the turn, even fall
in someone's lap—anyone, okay? Touch
elbow, knee, shoulder, it's called being alive.
The warning bell? Music to my ears. Math,
history, bio lab? Love it! Backs of heads
while teach gives a PowerPoint? Beautiful.
The hall at break, lockers slamming,
every body bumping into every body?
What's better than that, I mean really?
Better than these home walls and window.
Wish I was in class right now, staring
out the window wishing I was home.

Pandemic Press Conference

It's classroom style—the flag,
the lectern facing rows of chairs.
Someone's up front, in charge
of reporter-pupils with pens at ready.

A hand goes up, teacher points.
We see this scholar did the homework.
Her question goes to the heart—but
then he shames her, names her dunce.

Sometimes it's grad school—the fate
of the world at stake. Sometimes it's
kindergarten, and we all get
the lesson on bullying.

School was never quite this hard.
Recess never looked so good.

For a Daughter in Quarantine

It's all so like a dream as in my mind I drive
the empty streets to find you across the river,
turn east and north, all trees in wild blossom.
In my mind, I descend the steps to your
basement den—with food, drink, music.
We sit together, your stories and mine.

I'm old, may catch it, be gone. Or you . . .
or both of us. It was always possible, but
now we live in acceleration of the possible.
I always wanted your independence, and
now we have it—I here writing this,
and you there, in danger, brave.

Child, girl, woman—it's okay.
From far, we live this day.

Oregon Dawn in Spite of the News

Before I can get to the day's statistics—so
many stricken, so many dead—I'm summoned
by the birds raising a ruckus outside, crows
and jays in festive outrage, chirrr and aria

from the little brown birds, the mournful
dove, the querulous towhee, rusty starlings
in their see-saw mutter, and a woodpecker
flicker hammering the gutter staccato.

On the porch, I'm assaulted by the merciless
scent of trees opening their million flowers
as I inhale the deep elixir of hazel, hawthorn,
maple, and oh those shameless cherry trees.

And just when I've almost recovered
my serious moment, I gasp, helpless to see
the full queen moon sidling down
through a haze of blossoms.

Bird in Hand

Walking before dawn I found, under the streetlight,
a song sparrow hunched on asphalt looking about
unafraid, or somehow injured, where I crouched
to see the speckled breast and up-thrust tail, twig
feet, pert eye sizing me up, then turning away.

Across the river, a train wailed south, and under
lockdown the city hummed low, chastened, as in
all our thoughts statistics swarmed, predictions bristled,
cautions ruled, and we all fed on morsels of warning
as if on crumbs, until we were filled to bursting.

Under warm feathers I brought two hands together
to set you down at the grassy verge—but tiny feet
climbed my sleeve, whirring in a dusky blur
that brought the thought—if bats can have it,
pangolin, or tiger, why not you, my beauty,

fluttering along my arm to offer blessing
and warning in one light touch?

Do You Miss It?

A Catechism for Lockdown

Do you miss texting "I'll be a few minutes late"? Or
calling: "I've hit some traffic"? Thinking: "Does this
meeting matter?" Wondering: "Is this how it has to be?"

Do you miss east side errand, west side delivery, bridges
totally stalled? Idling in rush hour, blue smoke swirling,
talk radio percussive, circling the block for a parking spot.

Do you miss telling the boss, "That's my birthday,
but, okay, I'll be there." Telling a child, "Maybe
on the weekend." Telling yourself, "When I retire."

Impulse-buys online—hey, the money's rolling in.
Wondering what an eight-hour luxury sleep might be like.
Old friend encounter: "How's it going?" "Good . . . busy . . .

Great to see you, but I gotta go." Telling your friend,
over your shoulder, as you stride away, "Hey, let's
catch up . . . I'll call you . . . we'll find a time. . . ."

Will We Go Back, after the Vaccine?

When I taught poetry, back in the day, we'd gather
at a school parking lot after the kids went home,
compare accounts of rush hour, delays, close calls.
If the building was locked, I'd call the janitor, she'd come
shuffling her keys, we'd get in, find our room, circle
our desks, set out food, and books for browsing
or borrowing, and begin. We'd write and share—
our voices, our tears and laughter.

Now we meet online. No food, no books. Instead,
we're all in gallery view, each isolate screen showing
a grid of faces, then a poem on screen-view.
We talk, go mute, and write.

Fifteen cars don't drive across town. Fifteen parents
don't leave their children. Some hold up a glass of wine.
One plays her viola and we weep. The stories still
rise up in our good company. We relish the writing
together—our voices, tears, and laughter.

Inmate Calls Home

Mom, I been all night worried—
this virus thing, they say it gets everywhere.
So don't go out, okay? Get food, sit tight.
Read. Just read. You like that. Make calls.
Not like visits, I know. You love those friends.
Nights, I hear you tell them things, in my mind.

Mom, I been worried—cabin fever. Yeah, here
on the inside we're used to that. Lots of practice.
Time crawls like a broken dancer, you watch it.
But Mom, what you gonna do with all that time?
No visits, no go where you want, no bench
in that park you like.

Nights, Mom, no worry. No you worry,
okay? Me, I'm good. I'm so good.

**Pandemic Coffee
Restoration Ritual**

A heaping dose of darkness,
a narrow pour of light,
a ringing spoon of silver
transforming wrong to right.

Deep inside the darkness
let a glimmer be revealed,
a slender path ahead
to where we will be healed.

Dark and light together—
loving how they swirled.
Now you've had your coffee,
go repair the world.

Dr. Fauci's Smile

Now we live for the day
the good doctor can stand
at the microphone, his
furrowed brow softening,
a modern renaissance beginning
as a wistful Mona Lisa smile
slowly ghosts his face, and he
speaks the four-beat line:

We got through it.

What does it take to get there?
Shelter in place. Lead a simple life.
Learn how little you need.
Prepare to smile.

Shelter in Place

Long before pandemic, the trees
knew how to guard one place with
roots and shade. Moss found
how to hug a stone for life.
Every stream worked out how
to move in place, staying home
even as it flows generously
outward, sending bounty far.

Now is our time to practice—
singing from balconies, sending
words of comfort by any courier,
kindling our lonesome generosity
to shine in all directions like stars.

3.

Revising Genesis

I Am the Seed

Every chance I get, any place I fit,
in a cleft of grit, in ravine or pit
by ancient wit my husk I split—
    I am the seed.

I fell to the ground without a sound,
by rainfall drowned, by sunlight found,
by wonder crowned, by luck profound—
    I am the seed.

After fiery thief, after bout of grief,
though life is brief I sprout relief,
with tiny leaf, beyond belief—
    I am the seed.

I am the seed, small as a bead.
Tell me your need. Your hunger I'll feed—
any trouble you're in, I will begin,
for I am the seed!

Up I rise to seek the prize
from all that dies, by bold surprise,
before your eyes, small and wise—
    I am the seed.

Advice from a Raindrop

You think you're too small
to make a difference? Tell me
about it. You think you're
helpless, at the mercy of forces
beyond your control? Been there.

Think you're doomed to disappear,
just one small voice among millions?
That's no weakness, trust me. That's
your wild card, your trick, your
implement. They won't see you coming

until you're there, in their faces, shining,
festive, expendable, eternal. Sure you're
small, just one small part of a storm that
changes everything. That's how you win,
my friend, again and again and again.

Earth Totem

Dorsal cedar dressed in moss where the village stood.
Crest carved fresh and proud, the clan not yet defeated.
White on black the color of starlight, high and old.
Glittering where the sea's back breaks open. In the strait,
their formation ancestors could use to teach children
the ways of courage, certainty, persistence.

Thriving where King Salmon thrive, the throng
charging in their own endemic wave through waves,
splitting the eternal, binding what flows, braiding
salt to salt in a shape the old ones carved in stone,
up from the hidden, forth through the hungry,
diving, secret, swallowed by the sea.

Who will lead us into the future if not these?
Who will teach us high respect, if not
the whales that prey on whales? Who
among us can dance like that, in storm
or cold, driving through shoals of silver
where all the little lives glitter in beautiful fear?

Hold honor of ancestors in our keeping, destiny of children,
eel and clam, eagle and heron, bear and frog, all the woven
hungers nourishing us by their vigor, their abundant life.
How can we meet our children's eager, brimming gaze
if we let the orca essence falter, barren, hungry, gaunt, if
our pod of treasures dive, never to return?

Puddle Jumper

From above, you can chart migration maps of trouble
for every long-flyer beating north or south—duck,
hawk, swan, goose, swallow, tanager, wren—peering down
to the red-lit blur of roads, cities bristling blinding light,
interchange knot, tangle of wires tethered to slave trees,
ancient marsh gone to blacktop skin, the lacy skein of the river's
former wanderings now bound in a fast run—but there,
in a glittering seam somehow left beside the highway, two ducks
freighted with fatigue find a watery remnant beckoning, and veer
down in a stall, fall from the sky and splash a gash
into a patch of heaven.

Beside frenzied roads, between fields, in some margin forsaken
by human cleverness two pilgrim ducks in a ditch stitch one shred
of Eden to the next on their journey, wild refugees seeking
episodes of rest.

In spite of all we've done wrong, the beauty is this for duck
and hummingbird, for fox or mouse, owl or butterfly—there are
these lands yet wild in coalition that hold just enough in knit thickets,
meadows, prairies, lazy streams and brimming seams of earth,
refuge of a lone tree, forgotten field, a grove left standing
or a watershed somehow outside our busyness.

Human chance shall be judged
by two ducks from a ditch lifting off, flying high
to look down on what we've left for them,
          and for our own young kin.

Foolish Young Flowering Plum

It's winter—dark days, still too cold
for bird or blossom—dull sky,
and all our hearts in shadow.

But there—at a ragged cleft
darkened by cedars of gloom
a flash of light cries out—

the incandescent wisp of wild
plum—far too early to be
so happy, so naive, a child

refusing to obey the rules of grief.

Wild Birds Teach Us

1. How Birds Die
Get caught by a kitty cat: 2.4 billion.
Collateral damage of industry: 700 million.
Hit a window: 600 million.
Hit by car: 214 million.
Get poisoned: 72 million.
Hit a powerline: 25 million.
Get electrocuted: 5 million.
Hit a turbine: 234 thousand.
Get blinded by city lights and stray.
Search in vain for starlight's guide.
Get out of sync with climate change:
    depart too late, arrive too early.
Land in a lake of arsenic.
Get your wings fouled in oil.
Eat plastic. Eat foil. Eat lead shot.
Eat lead shot and have a seizure.
Eat poisoned insects and carry their doom.
Lose your acre of breeding ground, and so
circle the parking lot that was a marsh.
Circle and circle, cry and cry.
Be a snowy owl in the era of *Harry Potter*,
    caged by a reader, expected to prophesy.
Be the wild pet of seven billion mammals with hands.
Be the last one of your kind, singing and singing.

2. How Birds Live

Fence wire—a throne for singing and singing.
Thorns in the blackberry thicket—jewels of safety.
A vacant lot, rife with a chance mix—heaven.
Wing bars of crimson, mustard, moss—kinfolk.
A fat worm, a ripe seed, a caught beetle—enough.
Twig feet on a twig after a thousand miles—rest.
Bill tucked under a wing—spiral home.
Cast-off thread and thistledown—snug nest.
A silence into which to put a few water notes—duet.
Breeding season, egg season, fledgling season—destiny.
Wings in the mist riding, gliding—no trace.
Heart-surge song rising from inside—beauty's custodian.
A short, intense, breathless life—grace.

Revising Genesis

And God said, Rest here in the garden
where you belong, where now you know
the good from evil, and so the good may be
your calling. Be home here in beauty and bounty,
and by salt sweat of your close devotion, make Earth
your wise guide, each creature teaching miracles of being
in wing and song, in blurred heart of hummingbird
and deep thump of whale, counting nights
in peace and days in blessing, as you
raise your arms in praise.

Lessons from a Tree

Seed split. Root sprout. Leaf bud.
Delve deep. Hold fast. Reach far.
Sway. Lean. Bow. Loom.

Climb high. Stand tall. Last long.
Grow. Thicken. Billow. Shade. Sow seed.

Rise by pluck, child of luck,
lightning-struck survivor.

Burn. Bleed. Heal. Remember. Testify.
Nest. Host. Guard. Honor.

Fall. Settle. Slump.
Surrender. Offer. Enrich.

Be duff. Enough.

Now Every Weed Is Precious

In this extinction era, dandelions
sassy at the cracked curb illuminate
our chance. As the old gold hoard
of monarch butterflies, once bannering
the sky, dwindles to a few, I can't slap
the dusty miller. Where wren song
is gone, mosquito hums holy,
holy, holy, and a thread of moss
in any concrete seam spells
intricate salvation. I bow
to the pluck of life wherever
green leaves wag
or small wings beat.

At the Meadow Called
a Scab with Kendrick

It's a scab because the soil is thin.
Trees can't grow, so the sun owns it.
At the slope's top, a seep keeps sedges.
And after snowmelt, before drought,
the flowers go insane, blinding us where
crimson runners of wild strawberry
knit penstemon to paintbrush,
mariposa to yarrow, allium to gentian,
where bees, flies and butterflies dip and veer
in the swirl of pollen bannering
the sun, where deliberate bumblebees
tumble into cups of rouge, drunk
and heavy, freighted with wild sweet
as I am, weeping so I can't stop, the pang
of beauty doomed by human greed,
my own nectar of salt brimming
at the nexus of sorrow and resolve:

May my life be scab soil, spare but
buttoned with beauties of apprehension,
small joys strewn across desert days—older,
purer, ever more severe in savoring
and sustaining what will remain.

For the Toad by the Kitchen
Step at Haystack, 4 a.m.

Rain has come and life is good!
Everywhere in the dark forest,
in moss along my favorite path, and in
my den in duff, a hum of well-being!

Listen! Hear the tramp of the makers?
Percussive steps on bedrock, on the wood
stair, and earth! All that resonant thrum
of tinkering, as they chatter and blur.

How they long to make a jewel like me!
My pearled belly, magnificent articulation
of my toes, and the glory of my pebbled back
in colors subtle beyond imagining.

Oh, these humans, my towering kin
intent on fashioning their poor equivalent
of what a tree does, simply standing up,
or rain falling to perfectly dimple the sea,

or a toad content in Buddha pose.
In spite of all, I must forgive them.
If they don't tread on me, they'll make me
die with laughing, chanting every night.

Nuptial Flight

The big buzz drone has been
in a holding pattern up
sixty feet, waiting for days.

The virgin queen, svelte
honey-skin ballerina,
rises to his station.

Coupled, tumbling, giving
her seed enough for a life
of labor, he shatters into debris.

Heavy, she descends
to the hive lip, limps in,
begins to lay a thousand

every day, single mother dipping
abdomen into cell after cell, while
all around her dance their children.

Enough

Where the young river shattered over stones
we stood captive to the small dun bird bobbing
and trilling, chanting, surging song inside
water's booming bell where it gripped
a water hump sliding over boulders
in a sheen, then peering under, splitting
the flow to know below the shine
where caddis crawled. It dipped
and sang, we stood statue, tranced
by the wild water song feathered in gray,
and I felt—*enough*, that's enough this life
has been, coming to this.

But walking on along the frosted path
the wan sun made shine, I felt the old
greed come back—to feel more, to see
and savor more before I slip under
the lip of the visible to fly dark
waters into origin.

At the Farm

Once they asked me to watch over things
while they were away, just a few days of summer—
the sheep loose in their domain of tattered grass
and young trees, chickens scratching and worrying
their pen white with droppings, feathers, and corn.
See to the garden now and then, choose from the bin
of gloves on the porch a pair to fit me, and add
some polish to the hickory hoe handle.

But then they were gone down the dusty lane, it was
evening, and I realized no one had said what to do
with the moon rising heavy over the east field, or how
to manage the crickets chirring their shuttles through
thick dark, or why I should sleep in the house when
the barn loft was soft with hay and smelled like my
grandmother's life in the nineteenth century, and
when you lay down, the moon shot spindles of light
through shingle cracks above.

No one said that blessings could be counted.
No one warned me how the farm would take me
and shake me like a stick the dog got hold of,
set me down like thistle wisp at midlife
waiting for the next breath of wind to take me
forward into what I never guessed could be:
my happiness.

Beautiful Redundancy

Every willow leaf, aching into green
from its crimson stem, offers another lovely
imperfection among these millions along
the round-stone bank dressing clear streams
that are built of rain-seeds, all of like mind,
flowing so the water knife
may cut through mountains and whittle
sand pebbles the ants raise into their
glittering pyramid studded with blue flowers so
microscopic they bring me stunned to my knees
to whisper holy, holy, holy.

Why this profligate redundancy of beauties
everywhere I turn—the old leaf gone to lace,
the new sprout small as a comma
each seed hurls toward the sky?

Birdsong, rain-glisten, snail-whirl, butterfly
unfurling her spiral tongue—it must be
a kind of merciless democracy of beauties
voting for our attention, every child
open-mouthed in wonder.

To not see this is to die a little.
To not hear, not touch is to be tyrannized.
To not defend this is to be complicit
with sorrow, with fear, in betrayal of earth.

I say send your pleasure hungry forth
to be stunned by every leaf
from the crimson wand of willow
aching green.

Psalmon Berries

Old pioneer, writing his sister back in *Ioway*,
praised the great abundance of *psalmonberries*
in mud-footed thickets of spiny cane elk
shouldered through while wrens sang psalms
and salmon came clubbing up every stream
in such throngs their splashing thundered,
and you could pull rosy yellow thimbles
from stems bear-fashion with your lips
and tongue when time was young in Oregon.

Now we need those psalms and stories
as we cherish remnants that escaped our
busy greed, the fish-starved streams, scant saplings
dotting clear-cuts, asphalt over moss, wires
tangling the sky. For still, in a lucky ravine
wildcatters missed, this salmonberry thicket thrives
where you take the children to reach, pluck, taste,
and sing it: *Psalmonberry. Oh Psalmonberry.*

Midden at the Estuary

The new owners of the house above the river
hired a backhoe to bury fiber optic cable
so at the tideline, across from sunset, over
the glassy pool of the estuary sliding in and out,

under storms scudding inland and eagle circling
against the sun, in the pouch of fragrance from
woodsmoke and salt, tuned by wave roar, inside
the singing circumference of the winter wren

by day and owl by night, in the dim dusk lit
by June fern and rain, they could have internet—
to be connected, you know—but the hinged
bucket sheared through the hillside tangle

of alder and blackberry to expose the rotted
heap of mussel shell, deeper than a man, and
in the litter there I found someone's jawbone
with two teeth, and for a moment stared

through the veil of all we have lost
to see this mother stepping down the bank
to turn over the stones before me
where the tide has ebbed away.

Wonder's Wisdom

Starting early, all my teachers
stamped kinship with the wild
by introductions crowded small:

nectar bead from honeysuckle sipped,
grasshopper gentleman chewing tobacco,
clover stem nodding a honeybee—

tiny friends in fur and wing,
fierce eyes peering back
into my stunned wonder gaze—

butterfly tongue plunging into yellow,
ladybug pirouette on my pinkie tip,
snail's eyestalks unfurling—

so my own prehensile spirit
reached to the aura's touch
of every intimate in hand—

sow-bug roly-poly clasping writhing feet,
snake string ringing my wrist,
pussy-willow kitten petted with my nose—

breathless, earth-close,
hungry for small affections real
or imagined for cousins in all directions—

salamander raised-palm salute,
polliwog swirl in a dripping hand,
minnows flashing silver into shadow,

dragonfly's knitted streaks of light,
snapdragon's love-bite on my tongue,
grass whistle in a thumb prayer,

wooly-bear curled to sleep,
hummingbird blur and gone,
crickets chanting from dark hollows—

all that rustling in the thicket,
all those whispering stars,
my mother moon summoning:

Come from the house and see.

Do You Need Anything from the Mountain?

Could you bring me a smudge of camas blue,
and the whisper whistle of that one pine
at the edge of the meadow at dusk, when day

gives a lost, last breath? Bring me the road
that becomes deep duff as it trails away
into the forest, young firs ten feet tall

along the hump between the old ruts.
Bring me a story you hear in dark silence
after the last light, the gone that gathers dew

in the fingers not to hold, carry away, but
only to feel. Bring me that skein of fire
that hangs in intimate eternity, after

the dark but before the thunder, when
the bounty of yearning in one cloud
reaches toward another, in each being's

endless, impossible desire to complete itself
before falling away.

4.

The Cup No One Can See

Our Singer Come from Afar

for Naomi Shihab Nye

Be our wren or warbler lit in willow
swaying with your tender weight
of songs, sipping the sky to tell us
hard things from far away you
freighted for our understanding and
comfort. Sing the mysterious harmony
of news and blessing, hurt and healing
offered with head high, eye bright
until with a friendly shrug
you flit away and leave us
strangely younger.

Two Rivers

One river flows above ground—
everyone can see it shining
across the land, following the valley
and shaping the valley, never at rest.

And some people say, *I know who
you are . . . I know what you've done . . .
what you lost . . . where you came from . . .
where you are going. I know.*

But what do they know of you, really?
For another river flows below all that,
invisible, at the speed of a dream
inside you—intuitive, curious, innocent.

And you say, *I know who I want to be . . .
I know what I've learned . . . I know what I love . . .
I need to know who I really am.* So you remember,
you wonder, you write, you shape story,

and you say to yourself on the page,
*Hidden river, spill your secrets
at the wellspring. I hold forth
my cup no one else can see.*

Poetry in Prison

You're in, but the question is:
what's in you? What story
aching to be told do you hold
in solitary, shackled, denied
its rights to visitors?

The hard things that happened are gold
you hammer into shape, the pain
you twist, the grief you make shimmer,
the lost good thing you restore
by telling it back into being.

Everyone is in prison, one way
or another. And everyone is
free, one way or another. The trick
is to find your way to bear the story
forth, so it shines in a listener's eyes.

Lost & Found People

That's what Jamie called them,
when we met in prison
and he spoke of love: "There was
this great big woman," he said—
"big heart, trouble getting around,
so I helped her, we went to all
the homeless camps to round up
the First people, the Native people,
the Lost and Found people, got them
on this bus to the Sun Dance where
you have to bleed to make it
real, to let the Creator see you,
just look up into the sky, into
the sun, let go all the bad you've done,
stand on the ground, on the earth,
open your heart to who you are—
lost and found, lost and found,
I was lost and I was found."

Then Jamie was silent for a time.
There was a light around him
where he sat in that flimsy prison chair.
That light came from the woman he helped.
It came from the sun.
It came from his heart
first hurt when he was young.
It came from what he still has to do.
He carried that light. I carry it.
I give his light to you.

Connect the Dots

A veteran slumped in a midnight
doorway was trained to kill, so killed,
and killing banished sleep.

A hurt child, now thirty-two, who
never had the food he needed, haunted
by his father's blows, shoots meth.

A mother abused as a girl, can't
speak of it, shuns touch, can't trust
any boy her own girl brings home.

A nation, founded by the shot heard
round the world, prevailing at Hiroshima,
can't understand our daily massacres

as if a gun were not a war in small,
strife undeclared but flaring sudden,
as one thing becomes another.

A life of kind words and gentle gestures?
Planting seeds and seeking peace?
Where could that take us?

Wren's Nest in a Shed near Aurora

Three tiny eggs in thistledown
cupped in a swirl of grass
in the pocket of the tool belt
I hung on the wall of the shed
when it finally stood complete—
will be three songs
offering local dignity for
my country enthralled by war
in distant lands.
                Stand back
cautiously, close the door
tenderly, let the future
ripen, grow wings,
and build songs.

Midrash on a Sacred Encounter

When the little ones gathered at my feet
they couldn't stop laughing every time
I spoke a poem, as if they were wild birds
and I scattered seed for their singing and singing,
singing back to my songs and stories, and they
fed me questions old as psalms: *How long*
does it take to write a poem . . . what's the longest
poem . . . who taught you poems . . . what's
the oldest poem . . . what's oldest
inside a poem . . . what is a poem
and what is not?

Then they laughed and clapped
and I bowed and felt blessed
and we went forth to heal the world.

Poetry Class at the Women's Prison

Put chairs in a circle. "Where
is everyone?" "Oh, they're all
watching *Love After Lockup*.
It's fake, but addicting."

On every chair, put a notebook
and a pen. "You know what?
In this class I'm not an inmate,
I'm a person." "Every time

that door opens, and another
joins our circle, we're stronger."
"It's not so much what we write—
it's how we listen." Finally, the show

over, the room resonant,
we are the full twelve writing
in a ring, as onto scribbled pages
we bow to pray hard stories.

At the Bird Refuge on MLK Day

We met at the island to stand on the levee watching
young mergansers learning to fish, diving clean
to the invisible, turning in the dark to follow silver
flashes, then splashing back into the light—
he Black and I White sharing his binoculars
to understand life beyond the human.

We kept our voices low, so not to frighten
the lesson in survival we could witness there.
Behind us, all the marching, all the hurt, the hate,
prison, baton, fire-hose, dogs, the Selma bridge,
the strike, the bombing, Emmett, Edgar, Martin,

Before us, calm water, young life, a future.
And between us, back and forth, the lens
for seeing.

Seeking Abe at Cline Falls

Where the highway swoops the canyon
to cross the river and climb away, I slid
down road-cut scree to seek the bird man's
feral realm below the rim, where once he
smeared peanut butter on juniper trees
to stud with crushed corn so chickadee
or nuthatch could twinkle from his lips
a seed of sunflower, could grace his shoulder
as a bough hunched for perching.

Hermit saint, he told me of the inner-outer,
the force that pegged him to this ground, the tug
he sent to drag a magpie screaming down
to crash his hat and flurr its wings in thrill.
He flourished his bedside urine pot and asked me
if that dark tint meant trouble. He knelt by young corn,
bedded in manure from the horse barns he had carried
by night from farms above, where clean people
dwelt with their lights and plans.

Now Abe, his birds have sung to sleep, his
scrapwood hut in its halo of debris swept clean
away, trunks licked bare by birded generations,
his furrows, snaking through fallen stones
for corn, well plundered back to dust
by thirty winters. But I wonder somewhere
high in a juniper, if a pair of sassy magpies,
kin to his character, have knit their nest
with willow twigs and the steely hair of Abe.

A Blessing for Teachers:
My People, My Heroes, My Friends

You are a teacher because, helplessly,
you love the invisible future thinly disguised
as a child who does not yet know her power, his gift,
and it is up to you to create conditions where
these wonders may be revealed.

So, alchemy in a crowded room,
transmuting the lead of device-medicated torpor
to the gold of fevered engagement with the self,
each other, and the Earth—this is the mission
you have chosen to accept.

A teacher, you befriend the invisible future
by looking into the eyes of beginners, and there
find the glimmer, the shimmer, the glance outward
from reticence to a few words, from a few words
to a story bristling with thought.

Knowledge is a fossil we turn over in our hands,
but learning is this living water for the young
we ladle out by looking into the eyes
of the children entrusted to us
by the hard world.

Poetry Doctor

How do you feel?
How, exactly, have you
learned to feel—to be
touched, to apprehend?
These twinges you have—
of compassion, empathy, pain—
how long have you had them?
Have they grown more intense
with age? Do they manifest at
sunset? At dawn? In the presence
of beauty? Of suffering?
Does your heart ever skip?
Do you ever feel dizzy
with delight or shame? Has
the grace of a few right words
ever blurred your vision? Caught
your breath? Has your heart
ever become a drum when
a song's words told you
who you are in secret?

I'm afraid my diagnosis
must remain incomplete
without further tests:
Neruda, Dickinson, Basho.

Ostracon

I never really knew my mother.

Learning to tie my shoes was the beginning.

Consoled by the way rivers move.

A dream was never enough.

Making bread, I forgot you for a moment.

Sometimes at night, only breath.

Pain is a substance, a stain.

One sip, and I remembered.

My Wife Wakes Me at 3 a.m.
to Tell Me She Is Overwhelmed

Not for joy did we marry, but for this,
to hammer through the to-do list
in the dark, despair shared, one
to lament and one to listen, knowing
nothing can be done before dawn,
but still the quiet aria, fierce
prosecution of the self, as I say
what can be done will be done
in time. For soon the tide will turn,
days will bloom and fade, impossible
imperatives will shrink to their true size
for her, but rise as a tidal wave for me,
and in the night, cast down, I will be
the one lamenting to my bride
at the dark heart of my defeat
and she will tell me all is well
in this dance we do
for one another.

Letters to Strangers

Dear Vagabond under his bridge . . .
Dear Mother who lost her son . . . Dear
Soldier far from home, the weather
here is winter, and I think of you.
We lost those old summers when
we knew not what we would know.

Dear Deputy patrolling the graveyard
shift . . . Dear General holding the fate
of children . . . Dear President with
the red phone of destruction, we
need you to feel pain, know
love, cherish kinship.

Dear Driver on a long road . . . Dear
Grandmother waiting for a call . . .
Dear Young Girl walking alone
through light snow, if the road
never ends, if the call never comes,
if the quiet snow grows ever deeper,

then I pray this letter may reach you
so in your pocket you will have
this message from your cousin, your
brother, your friend. Though far, we
are alive together, you and I—under
the bridge, and on the snowy road.

Words You Learn to Serve the American Dream

"May I help you?"
"Just one?"
"I'll be your server."

"Did you say 'Fill up'?"
"Credit or debit?"
"Do you need a receipt?"

"Room service."
"Do you need new towels?"
"Will that be all?"

"Yes."
"Whatever you want."
"Right away."

"Reporting for duty—sir!"

Sunset North from Gold Beach

At the turn-off, the road kinks back on itself,
finds a way under 101 to dead-end at the beach
where waves pound sand, where the creek
pools before surrendering to the sea.

Walk with me south to where the sand ends
in rockfall, the mountain coming apart, its
strata shattered where the waves keep licking
at its feet, persistence winning over certainty.

Above the high-tide line, we lift a run of kelp,
once fluid in the deep, now pale and dry in curl,
spiral, and figure-eight to map the changes we have lived—
no straight path ours, but this kink of loss and luck.

Remember when we thought our jobs would last? Remember
when we thought we would be four, instead of three?
Remember your father's silent passing, my mother's
final night? Beloved, knot your hand in mine.

The sun sinks, flares, winks out.
Our road goes winding on.

The Candle Burning
in the Photograph
on Pilar's Office Door

The wick grows dusky
as the flame burns bright.

We know the feeling,
you and I—reciprocal

diminishing and brimming
steadily at once.

How could it be otherwise
as fire opens the fisted cone

before rain can loosen earth
for the seed to raise a flag?

We do our teaching, asking
everyone to breathe, to listen.

The candle gives all it has,
growing short as light goes far.

Song after Ishiguro

There was another life I might have had,
but I am having this one.

— *Kazuo Ishiguro*

To glimpse the roads I never walked—
my heart begins to spin.

I carry wayward stories
of all that might have been.

If I were starting over
would I take this life again?

Can I savor satisfaction
for all I hold within?

Win or lose is not the game—
with every breath *begin.*

Those were the lives I might have lived,
but this is the one I'm in.

For the Woman Picking Litter from the Beach

Her task is vast—in fact,
impossible, so why is she
humming as she snatches
plastic bits from drift wrack
all along the high-tide line?

Glum lovers pass, their world
of finite joy already waning,
while her future is filled
with a clear calling ahead
and a clean set of tracks behind.

5.

And All My Love

The Fact of Forgiveness

It is a given you have failed.
It goes without saying you were hurt
        and so you hurt some others.
Of course you alone could have saved someone
            or something you did not.
The midnight court of the sleepless mind
        has reached its verdict: Life Sentence.
Life will be long and hard, but also mysterious
        in how you are condemned to live
        by beauty all the same.
Through the bars of your cell, you must watch
        the moon grow full and generous.
A tune made for others will arrive at evening,
        smuggled into your mind as if for you.
The world can't keep its treasures from you—
        no matter how little you deserve,
        you have it all:
Moon, Sun, Sleep, Waking, Water, Air—
        a bird dancing away out of sight
        leaving the print of its flight
        and a filament of song
        for you.

Dew & Honey

Sip by sip in thimble cup
the meadow bees will drink it up
then ferry home to bounty's hive
flowers' flavor, hum and thrive
to show us how through word and song
by gesture small and patience long
in spite of our old foolish ways
we may fashion better days.

So, my friend, come sip and savor
syllables as crumbs of pleasure—
by honor in each conversation
we begin a better nation.

Chores of Inspiration

for Dorothy Wordsworth

Attend to scales of herring on a moon-
wrinkled tarn, a writhing copse
of hazel in storm. Then darn
a ragged poem unto fair copy

for your brother while he sleeps.
Scrawl your recollection of silver
wrought by wet and light
on the backs of sheep in high fields

and give him this when he
wakes. Let him suffer
the burdens of fame, while
for you stillness offers treasure

of rivulet, first leaf, last light.

What We Did Before Radio

Before you go, say a few words. The world
gave you voice—*cry, whisper, laugh, hum.*
In silence at the window sometimes you

didn't know what to say, and then in school
they asked what you had almost learned.
Birds called down to you, wind teaching

through bare winter trees, rain tapping the code
for joy. Underground, or inside your heart
a stream was chanting. You took a little dipper,

sipped, and some words began for you. For this,
the world gave you voice. Before you go,
come down like an angel to laugh

inside a child's mind. Invisible
everywhere, be the one singing.

Quiet Day

Dawn day. Gone gray.
No car. No key. No place to be.
No task. No mask. No fancy shoes.
No news. Nothing to lose.
No greeting. No meeting.
A quiet nook. A long look.
No call. No knock. Forgotten clock.
Singing birds. Few words. Taking stock.
Dusk slow. Moon glow. Let go.

My Father's Hands Said No

Growing poor, my father took his short hoe
to the sugar beet fields—with that scant handle,
any boss could see if someone stood to rest.

My father's hands held the cheater bar
to cinch a mean valve at the refinery
where a spark could kick foul air to fire.

My father's hands plundered hollows
in the bank of the Ninnescah in search
of catfish, but a muskrat bit his thumb.

In war, my father held *Whitman* to his heart
when the mob in Arkansas shouted *Get a rope!*
to lynch him for refusing to kill.

His hands held the star drill, shivering
as a burly roustabout swung the sledge
inches from my father's head—*Almost*

killed a guy . . . this way once . . . missed my stroke . . .
laid him out . . . threw him in m'car . . . he sat
up, said . . . 'What happened?'

Instead of guns all through the war
my father's hands gripped hickory handles
of axe or spade or Pulaski, on his knees

to set young trees in earth, or stand
at the line to fight fire, or fling gravel from
a ringing shovel's blade as the crew built roads

we would travel after the fighting stopped
for a time, after that big bomb other hands
had built, hoisted into a plane, and with

a touch, let go. My father's said we could
live without weapons but with words—and
left me with an axe, a shovel, and the syllable No.

Aunt Mar Changes How We See

She had taken to having naps
most afternoons in the side parlor
while the TV flickered, muttered
brash fuss or hush of snow

as the long hours rounded into dusk,
so dear Mar, when we found her,
lay settled in the easy chair where her
soft light had stepped to the window,

slipped free through the cold clear panes,
passed lively into the buds of cottonwood,
her whispered "Yes" to wind and stars,
her way with folding hands, learned young

by lasting through the thirties, by raising nine
alone, by dealing books to hungry eyes in school,
by feeding us on the stove named Detroit Jewel,
her winsome prayers at times both hard and good

gone deep to the loyal roots of hickory, her calm
to elm reaching over the long prairie road
that joins the there of her
to the here of us, until it all

turns inside out, and through the world
beyond all trouble to core affections, no matter
how far or strange, we now see our days
by the gentle gaze of Mar.

How I Came to Be

The story goes that my father, a pacifist in the Good War,
was held at a camp in the California mountains where
a minister brought his pretty daughter to help attract the boys
to the Lord, but my father asked her to walk into the hills with him.

Evening, the lingering decrescendo of the sun, and the moon hung low.
They saw dust along a distant road. One began, "I have come upon a stretch
of dusty white road . . ." and the other said, "drinking up the moonlight
beside a blind wall . . ." and both knew the Willa Cather story where
this sentence lived, and knowing that, they recognized one another
to be kin to the story "Two Friends" in *Obscure Destinies*.

After a few days, back home in LA, she sent him a telegram
the war censor sent back to her, thinking it code: "After long thirst,"
she had written, "a draught of perfect good."

Imagine you are in a war, far from home, very poor, maligned,
long at a loss. Someone you have just met offers a few consoling
words from home. Would you not say, as he did, "Isn't this the way
it should be"? Would you not say, as she did, "But you don't know if
I can cook"? And in such coded words begin to knit the world
$\qquad\qquad\qquad\qquad$ together once again?

Blue Brick from the Midwest

After my father collapsed like a bolt of light, toppled without a word,
I was the one to enter his study, find the jagged note to our mother he
scratched as he reeled, the freight train of his departure hurtling
through his heart—

and will my love

—a sentiment he did not speak in seventy-nine years as tough customer,
affable but stern, inert when grief came, reserved as granite
when my brother died, cracking plaintive jokes when we trembled
in the hospital, mother going under the knife.

His way was trenchant, oblique. He distrusted those who
talk about God, preferring to honor the holy with a glance,
a nod, or silence. Delving deeper, the day he died, we found
in his sock drawer, under that scant set of flimsy raiment, the fetching
photo of the flirt: our mother, coy at the sink, looking back
over her shoulder, dressed only in an apron with a big bow.
No fool like an old fool.

And delving deeper, at the back of the bottom file (the niche
where one would hide the stuff of blackmail) I touched the blue
brick of love letters our mother had sent him when they
courted in the war—brittle leaves kissed snug together

and bound with string, the trove he had carried
in secret through every move since 1943. She knew
them not, nor had his. "Oh, Billy," she said.

Father, early years taught your way with the heart's contraband
when the dirty thirties blunted your bravado, tornado snatched
your friends, the war your tenderness, and left you with these secrets
hoarded for us to find when you were gone.

Emily's Barefoot Rank

She knew success, publication, fame
jeopardized the pencil stub
in pocket, old envelope
taking the heart's licked fire
beyond sight through
incandescent nights, skirmishes
of solitude and fevered union
kindled in the breathless mind.

Better step the side path
chanting hymns for cricket and grief
while the heedless world marches into dust.

Atavistic Memory

In a previous life I must have been
a woodsman, for pine scent thrills.
Or was I the hunter's apprentice,
bowing to read the deer's print
in dust? Cook's helper, master
of the broom—how sweeping
soothes my mind? Whistle punk,
leaping from danger. Gandy
dancer of singing rails. Silk in
my fingers takes me weeping
to my harem cell. Being beggar's
daughter prepared me to be
consoled by one coin's glint,
rain in a tin cup sipped,
the flavor of a nibbled seed.

My Brother Visits, 1988

The last time I saw my brother
he stayed at the little house
where I lived alone.
We walked to the park.

We sat together with tea.
He did not speak of his troubles.
But in the night, I heard him
crying. I held him in my arms.

I said I would take care of him,
but he said it's alright. He could do it.
In the morning, he was gone.
But on the window sill, a note

with his crooked words
in a cramped scrawl
I could barely read:
Thanks for the good times.

Curse of the Charmed Life

Things pretty much worked out for you—
you have what you need, and if you need more,
you have people ready and able to provide.

Sure, someday your luck will run out,
you'll be helpless, then gone, and your people
will gather in your honor.

There will be music, and tears. People will
embrace—for you. There will be an odd
buoyancy, a chatter of kind words, blessing.

But the curse of this charm is exile
from the unlucky, how gifts make you
deaf to the sudden shout

of a man camped in the ravine,
make you blind to the dirty face
of a woman with a cardboard sign.

Without hunger, it's easy to be heartless.
Without hurt, you are disabled. Without
the battering of bad luck, the pummeling

of lost hopes, the wounds of life without love,
of dark dreams that last past dawn, how can you
know what one life might do for another?

Stories from Dr. Zeus

Agamemnon, toddler, thwacking
thickets with his sword stick.

Before betrayal fostered fury,
Medusa snatching garden snakes.

Ariadne's goat wool spinning
plucked from thorns.

And the Calypso girl sending her
dreamy gaze far over the waves.

Old Dog

Brain tumor, the vet says—see how
she tilts her head, how her left leg sags?
See how she doesn't raise her muzzle,
but turns up her gaze to see if you
still love her? She could last a month, two—
or six? I've seen six. She'll tell you when
it's time. For now, it's just *Good dog.*
You're a good, good girl! See?
Tail still thumps. Maybe six!

A Note Stuffed through Our Car's Shattered Window, Passenger Side, at Stockton and Vallejo

Sorry someone did your window, man—these
guys, sometimes they just need to see what's
behind that tinted glass, you know? Like they
wonder how the rich folks do it, touch the leather.
Or maybe they have to punch a window instead of
a person, right? Like busted glass is a fix to get fury
out through the elbow so no one gets hurt. Like say
his lady called it quits. Now he got no place. Or maybe
his dad hit him so much, he's full of hits. Or the army
taught him to be tough, but not how to be who
he is, after. Or maybe he did this job, kind of
had it made, then poof! He's out. Starting over.
Has to figure the whole puzzle from zero.
Blow a hole through that.

But then maybe he saw your guitar in there,
and in spite of all that trouble, he left it, because
his dad used to sing sometimes, when he was sober,
or with his brother, and that's a line
you don't cross.

But hey, you can fix a window. Easy to fix a window.
A few connections, a few tools. Country's full of junkyards,
junkyards full of windows, all you need. In fact,
I know a guy—Ernie, 415-FIX-PANE.
They call him Window Man. Specialist, independent,
years in the business. He's a great guy.
Trust me. I know he'll make it right.

Before the MRI

Do you have a pacemaker?
Do you have an implanted cardio defibrillator?
Do you have a programable shunt?
Do you have a deep brain stimulator?
Do you have metal in your eyes?
Do you have tattoos, piercings, a toupee?
Do you have permanent makeup?
Do you have bullets or shrapnel
        under your skin?

Empty your pockets: no phone,
        no keys, no change.
Lie down on this bed.
Enter this tunnel.
Close your eyes.
It will be loud.
Good Luck.

What For?

What is beauty for—
sunset searing my soul
without thought or plan?

Dawn green beauty, bee hum honey,
stone in hand so silky the long sea
worked centuries to ravish?

And what for pain—thorn
in heart for my hurt child,
dumb ache for my brother gone

thirty years, slow burn of disgrace
when I fail at what I am to do: to see
my country bruised and torn?

So, to make good things—
a song, a kind act, a friendship—
feed on beauty at every turn.

And to make truth, feed on sorrows,
gnash their salty structures,
bite the bitter rind.

Outside My Window

The hummingbird arrived again
to taste the hearts of yellow flowers
spangled on the bush drought withered—
brave flowers, emerald epiphany,
the messenger in jeweled cape
a whirl, a blur of promise.

When you are gone, I see you
like that still, my brother,
my father and my mother flinging
pollen and tears in one lit
circumference wheel.

Easy Pickings

It's easy to laugh in the blueberry field,
staccato plink and plunk as berries plummet
into the pail, and you hear children banter
in a dozen languages among the green rows.

It's easy to forgive there, too—
viewing old betrayals sweetly diminished
by the honeyed crush of berries
on your tongue.

It's even possible to imagine peace
between people who hated each other
before their children met between these rows
and asked one another, "Shall we pick together?"

Come pick with me, my enemy, my angry self,
come, split couple bickering over money,
come to the blueberry field, Palestine and Israel,
come bow and squint under the sun-splashed leaves,

come peer into these dark shadows for blue.

Afterword

Many of these poems came to the page while I served as Poet Laureate of Oregon, 2018–2020, a calling that took me to the far corners of my native state to share the mysteries of words and stories. This work was informed by something said by my predecessor in this role, the Navaho-Wasco poet Elizabeth Woody: "The more I do this, the less it's about what the poem *is*, and the more it's about *who* the poem *serves*." The idea of a poem written *for* someone, or for a place, for an idea, for a cause—this perspective seized my imagination and led to the writing of poems for members of my family ("My Brother Visits"), for a stranger I admired ("For the Woman Picking Litter from the Beach"), for my teachers ("A Blessing for Teachers"), for immigrants ("Dear Mr. President"), for endangered whales ("Earth Totem"), for students at a little school ("Midrash on a Sacred Encounter"), for inmates at prisons ("Poetry at the Women's Prison," "Poetry in Prison," and "Two Rivers"), for wild creatures ("Wild Birds Teach Us"), and for the people in my beloved and restive country ("White Flag Patriots," "The Flavor of Unity," and "Old Glory's Red, Black, and Blue").

Another notion behind these poems is the distinction I see between a "great" poem and an "important" poem. Donald Hall once asked, "Why write poems if you can't write great poems?" Yes, perhaps . . . but it seems to me that view only goes so far. A *great* poem may be written by someone who is dead, and it gets into an anthology, and students are forced to analyze it to prove their worth as thinkers in the factory of academe. Great poems need scholars to footnote their hidden meanings and fame to spread their authors' names. That's all fine, I say. There are many great poems I love. But I am also drawn to *important* poems, which are utterances written as a local act of friendship or devotion, and given to a person, shared at an occasion, or performed in support of a cause. Such poems, often labeled "occasional verse," can be considered a lesser form of literature, an expendable artifact of the moment. This view privileges elite readers in far times and places over the direct and humble but essential exchange of thoughtful language as an inducement to deeper relationships now, to stronger communities, and a better nation in an interdependent world. Some poems in this spirit here include "Puddle Jumper" (written for the Coalition of Land Trusts), "Repeat Offenders" (written for a benefit for the homeless in my city), "Song after Ishiguro" (written for a friend in mourning), "Equinox" (written after reading about the child activist Greta Thunberg), and "A Note Stuffed through Our Car's Shattered Window" (written to cheer myself up after an act of vandalism in San Francisco). With that last poem, I began with lament, but was laughing out loud as I wrote the closing lines, once I recognized the voice composing the note. The poem changed my day and may have changed my life: You turn your gaze a few degrees and your chance for good luck and a buoyant outlook grows greater.

Are such poems limited to the occasion of their utterance, or do these occasions offer a chance for texts of expansive value to be born and to travel far beyond their moment? My father used to say that "All poems are local—somewhere." And I would say all poems arise from an occasion—sometime: a moment of creative crisis, wordless struggle, defeat, or epiphany. This view characterizes the poems in the second section, drawn from a series of "pandemic poems" I wrote and posted daily on Instagram for the contagion's first two months.

Beyond these distinctions, the poems in this book are essentially footnotes to the inexpressible, where words do what they can't say. As several have said in various ways, prose tries to explain what can be said, while poetry seeks to convey what can't be said. Poetry is a speaking silence, a musical nudge, a glance between intimate friends.

So I offer these glimmerings to you.